Rehearsal

Rehearsal

Kay Meier

Writer's Showcase
San Jose New York Lincoln Shanghai

Rehearsal

All Rights Reserved © 2002 by Kathryn M. Meier

Writer's Showcase
an imprint of iUniverse, Inc.

For information address:
iUniverse, Inc.
5220 S. 16th St., Suite 200
Lincoln, NE 68512
www.iuniverse.com

ISBN: 0-595-21179-8

Printed in the United States of America

for Fred Meier

Many have contributed to this book:
my parents Kathryn and George Schuette, my numerous teachers
and poet friends, especially Marc Frazier. I also want to
thank Margaret and Bill Atkins for their help with the text.

Acknowledgments

Amaranth Review. "Girl Child."

Blue Mesa. "Remnants."

Bristlecone. "Legends."

Cumberland Poetry Review. "The Falling Day."

Dominion Review. "South Portugal."

English Journal. "My Parents at the Century of Progress, 1933," "Belle of the Bay Islands," "Finalist," "Sequences," "My Inheritance."

Gryphon. "Rehearsal."

Karamu. "What Do We Know About the Universe?," "Black December, Bitter Dawn," "The Defiant Rose."

New Press. "Hotel Palmilla."

Oyez Review. "The Day My Mother Killed the Rose."

Piedmont Literary Review. "Island Boy."

Pleiades. "How the Past Is Lost."

Passages North. "Ruins."

Rhino. "Cairo, City of the Dead."

-2-

Slipstream. "Roomers, 1940's."

Sow's Ear. "Marriage in Three Acts."

Slant, Passager. "Forty Years After Their Death I Invite My Parents to Dinner."

The Sun. "Mother Versus Polio."

West. "Block House."

Whiskey Island. "Ceremonies."

Z Miscellaneous. "Definition."

Contents

PART THREE

Part One

Speaking of marvels, I am alive together with you.

Liseal Mueller

Forty Years after Their Deaths, I Invite My Parents to Dinner

My mother, her hair in a soft bob,
wears a string of pearls, pearl earrings,
a blue dress patterned with half moons.
She holds the arm of a slight man
in shirt sleeves. He smokes a Camel.

Dressed in a suitcoat and slacks,
I guide them into my living room
of glass, skylights and leather,
African masks arranged on the walls.
My mother says she remembers me
in a pink chiffon prom dress;
George, who died first, talks
of first communion, a white veil, prayer book.

He asks about Peabody Coal Company
but it went bankrupt thirty years ago.
Inquiring about the President,
he says if he had only voted for Al Smith instead of Hoover,
we wouldn't have had the Great Depression.
He wants to know how the war is going.
The last battle he remembers is Dunkirk.

-4-

My mother inquires about the antique locket
Dad gave her on their silver wedding anniversary.
She remembers our third floor walk-up,
its amber lights, prickly mohair furniture,
oak tables, heavy Venetian blinds,
those summer nights we sat outside.

She stops talking. I mention I live thirty miles
out of town. A clock chimes the hour.
They sit ramrod straight on the couch,
ready to leap up at a moment's notice.
My mother twists a Kleenex between her fingers.
My father puts out his cigarette in his hand.

The Falling Day

My mother loves the movies.
She is mesmerized by the passion and pain
of Gable and Lombard who live
on the screen at the Plaza theater
Sunday afternoons. As supper time approaches,
my father and I, grown eager for her return, dump pick-up-sticks
into a maze of color on the rug.
We snake each stick out
as if the world depends on it.

I remember sepia as if that room
were seen through a brown lens:
oak tables, mohair sofa, the Motorola,
one circle of light from a tall table lamp,
my father's thin body twisted toward the radio
when she arrives, wisps of hair straggling
from her cloche. He loosens her coat.
They lean together that December dusk,
the seventh day,
1941

The Day My Mother Killed the Rose

The last time she laughed
was before the phone rang one Saturday afternoon.
Then she didn't say anything.
Later she broke
her favorite trinket, a red rose
enclosed in a crystal globe.
She held a fork, tapped the glass gently
again and again until it cracked,
and liquid seeped across the oak table.
"I'm paying you back," she said to my father.

Block House

He lives in movable rooms,
at times placing them end on
end, building a tower, a mountain
to climb

or heaving the cubes to scatter like rocks,
rubble in leaves, a hallway here, an attic there,
he finds them, a sleepwalker finding his bed.
He carries the kitchen home, old pots scoured
bright, swinging on hooks.

Sometimes the rooms are clustered,
edges touching, locks carefully turned,
windows snug against any wind.

This keep will stand.
Occupants come to stay, no casual idols
to be tossed like yesterday's bouquet,
one black-white cat, the same dog,
no new wife.

Rehearsal

The winter she was twelve,
she became an old hand at losing.
First her mother died, then her father,
her grandmother in March.

She got used to black silk,
sermons, the reading of the will.
Neighbors would touch her arm,
invite her to dinner.

She was a carrier, spreading death,
prepared for two-faced girlfriends,
boys who didn't call back.
She could handle anything
but a promise.

-9-

Lena

She comes on Wednesday for the day,
exotic in our world with cropped hair,
circle earrings, armless flowered dress.

I watch as she washes my underwear in the kitchen sink,
arranges panties on a radiator,
scrubs the brown cement floor on her knees.

My mother is propped by pillows,
skin sallow against a cerise bed jacket.
Lena vacuums around the bed, lifts an end with one hand.

Mother's voice guides Lena through her tasks,
the same voice that prepares me for life without her.
Lena jokes in broken English. Both women laugh.

-10-

Sex Education

She knows the nuns will skip specifics
so she gives me a book with pictures and diagrams: arrowed labels
of glans penis, scrotum, testis, prepuce,
functions explained in three syllable words.

She calls me to the kitchen,
speaks slowly, determinedly.
I nod to show I understand,
not understanding.

"Don't ever let a man
get It in you,"
she says, looking at the wall.

-11-

Mother Versus Polio

By midsummer, cases number in the hundreds.
Doctors fight about the cause: air, water, Lake Michigan?
The *Trib* is filled with photos of babies in iron lungs,
Sister Kenny applying hot packs to paralyzed limbs,
youngsters struggling on crutches.

Mother scrubs apples, potatoes,
peels the skin from peaches, grapes,
insists on three baths a day, parsley juice at noon.
Inside our stifling apartment,
quarantined from playground or Plaza Theater germs,
I watch friends hurry home in wet bathing suits.
I live for "Jack Armstrong: All American Boy" on WLS.

One morning I wake with a rowboat stomach, fever.
Fifty years, but I remember that plunge into an icy tub,
the creak of her chair beside the bed
as we wait for my legs to turn to wood.

Girl Child

I. Anna

The widow made Anna quit school in the sixth grade,
set her on a high stool to make change,
while she worked the black soda fountain,
joking with men about cards in the back drawer.
Anna learned Rum and Maple, Bull Durham, Copenhagen.
She marked the seasons by the greeting cards
they sold. Santa Claus meant snow,
next came a flower cross, then wedding bells.

When they threw him out of school, Jim played
"twenty-one" in the back of the store,
dipped into the register every day.
Good Friday a heart attack took him,
coins falling across the glass counter, dice.
After his funeral, the widow mumbled to herself.
Anna threw away the greeting cards and
sold the fountain for a hundred dollars.

-13-

II. The Widow's Photo Album

Never her fault: the camera,
the film, bright sun, dim light.
Some bodies have no heads. Severed arms
reach from anonymous trunks.
One photograph slices Anna
as she serves birthday cake.

Toys and a silver Christmas tree.
Jim playing trucks, holding kittens,
catching a baseball, balancing on new skis.
She gets him centered: a hundred clear poses.

-14-

III. Anna Speaks

I ordered the hearse to circle past
the barred door of the store.
Even on Christmas she opened
for regulars wanting two cigarettes
for a penny.

Twice I signed the half-sheet of paper,
first for her right leg,
then for the left.
The doctors peeled away gangrene
like wilted lettuce.

She left everything to Jim,
but it goes to me,
my name not even in the will.

My Parents at the Chicago World's Fair, the Century of Progress, 1933

July, hot and they walk by the Japanese pavilion.
She wears a loose dress
that almost hides her first pregnancy.
Her hair is brown, windblown; she is not young,
he holds her arm:

a slight man in shirt sleeves, straw hat,
smoking. His mouth is too large.

They stop to read the 200 foot Haviland thermometer:
ninety. They buy chocolate cones, laughing.

He hires a rickshaw; they disappear
into the streets of Paris, ignoring a fortune teller's booth
where tea leaves might have revealed

that she is destined to wander through haunted midnights,
and he to die at fifty, discredited, alone.

Part Two

What do we know about the universe and how do we know it?

Stephen W. Hawking

What do we know about the universe and how do we know it?

for Stephen W. Hawking

Olduvai

I kneel in the dirt of the crater,
sweep the soil with a toothbrush.
At each turn of my wrist a hundred years falls away.
A jawbone appears. It may be the skull
of a woman who carried water from a well,
who saw her babies ravaged by disease,
watched men go off to war.

-19-

Giza

Inside the pyramid I hold a midnight vigil.
The spirit of Isis enters me,
whispers of assassins hired to murder her son,
to steal his golden treasure.
Egyptian faces stare wide-eyed,
full lips closed in stone.

-20-

Marrakeesh

In the market, snake charmers tame cobras.
Musicians stroll. Acrobats somersault.
Veiled women bargain for pieces of bloody lamb.
I know the spicy smell of their kitchens,
the stories they tell their children,
their secret dreams.

-21-

Chichen Itza

The feathered serpent demands sacrifice.
I hear the screams at the ball court,
walk beside a murky cenote where children drowned.
When jaguars roamed the jungle,
babies' heads were flattened by binding them to boards.

Yellowstone

Murmuring prayers to the earth gods,
an aged Indian woman weaves baskets.
She says her mother taught her
to butcher three buffalo a day,
to grind corn while men hunted.
Her own sons wander dark streets.

How the Past Is Lost

In the first picture a thin man with too many teeth
wearing high boots and knickers, cavorts
with a white dog, dark markings around its eyes.
The date is April, 1913, twenty years before I am born.

Men fish from a dock, holding poles long as balance bars.
My father links arms with three buddies
and a comely girl, her hair in a cap.
No one can tell me their names.

Before water my mother poses in a long skirt, her hair mussed by wind.
The background has almost disappeared,
but in my father's tiny writing: "Kitty—Wilson Beach."

She sits in a cane rocker
dressed in a flowered gown, high buttoned shoes.
The outlines of her face remain.
I can barely read "Our First Home—1913."

Chicago Blood

I

My Irish grandfather captains a fireboat on the River.
When he disappears for days,
his wife searches the bars in Back of the Yards,*
drags him home like a stray animal..
In a sepia photograph, she stares ahead grimly.

The German grandfather hides behind spectacles,
a handlebar mustache over his mouth.
He splits diamonds on State Street,
marries one woman after another. Three wives die in childbirth
before he goes bankrupt and succumbs to syphilis.

-24-

II

Bowtie anchoring a skinny neck, straw hat slanting over eyes,
my father swaggers down Montrose Beach.
On an impulse he leaps on to a rock over the water,
teeters back and forth.

Laughter explodes.
Narrowly avoiding a fall, he looks back,
finds her the color of peacocks.

-25-

III

My father inherits the family sex drive
but wants a good woman for his wife.

Nights my mother pushes by drunks.
She marries as soon as she can

but almost dies in the flu epidemic
while he waits on a troop ship that never leaves.

They move to a colonial in Beverly.
No liquor sold in the village.

-26-

IV

Fake references, fake diploma.
He lands a job thirty floors above LaSalle Street.
Camel between his lips, he balances the books at Peabody Coal,
wears a miner's cap, coveralls for trips down the shaft.

Vacations he sails Lake Michigan,
capsizes off North Avenue Beach one windy day.
My mother waits, wrapped in blankets.
When he reaches the shore, she runs to warm him.

-27-

V

About the time Capone's gang guns down seven men in a garage,
I am born via Caesarian section.
Afterward my mother develops mystery ailments
that confound doctors.
My father works late, spends steamy hours
in the arms of downtown prostitutes.

-28-

VI

He rages against circumstance
that makes him miss another war.
He wants to pilot a flying fortress,
storm Normandy, play desert tag with Rommel.

In a shirt pocket, he begins to carry the nitroglycerine tablets
that won't be enough to save his life
after he runs up five flights of steps one icy December day.

-29-

VII

I discover he was cremated at Graceland Cemetery* near the Lake
about the time I take the kids there on a field trip,
In my class is a curly haired descendent of Al Capone.

Back of the Yards*—the Chicago Stockyards—huge pens for holding and
butchering cattle.
Graceland Cemetery*—a Chicago cemetery where dignitaries such as
Marshall Field, Lorenzo Taft and Louis Sullivan are buried.

-30-

Lovers, 1942

While her parents fish hidden walleye holes,
Marge and Joe spend hours in her single bed.
Her scrubbed cleanness blinds him like noon sun.
His strong arms cradle her heart.

Now they wait in sleepy Wisconsin dusk
at a ramshackle train station.
The Northwestern swallows his khaki,
speeds him from the tasks of the seasons
to study weapons, how to kill.

Marge studies war news along with English lit,
hardens her body loading shocks of wheat,
drives a corn picker across the fields.
She visualizes children with her figure, Joe's height and good skin.

Her face flickers in the crosshairs of his bomb sight.
Crouched in the nose of the B17, his deft fingers play knobs
to neutralize the yawing of the plane.

While he sleeps in the belly of the bird,
anti-aircraft rips the fuselage.
Years will pass before Marge leaves the farm.

My Inheritance

does not include the
the sound of my father's voice.
Nine years to remember
delicate hands, a thin face
with too many teeth,
eyes only from photographs,
eyes without light.

His work was ciphers, columns
of numbers. He'd sit and smoke,
reading Ernie Pyle, living each invasion.

I only saw the bedroom door closed twice.
Am I dreaming striped pajamas.

A kiss on the moist forehead.

Black December, Bitter Dawn

Mother pushes me up icy stairs
to the deserted Division Street Platform.
Billboards tout toothpaste, cigarettes, whiskey.
I put my hands into one pocket of her seal coat,
wonder about my father, the 5 A.M. phone call

We shiver on yellow cane benches,
bump each other with every jolt.
The car lurches forward, trembles on the edge.
I imagine it falling to the street,
bodies spilling out like rag dolls.

Chimneys and rooftops take shape.
In hidden rooms, lives flicker.
At Mercy Hospital, my father lingers.

In the Balcony of the Palace

Air conditioning replaces the furnace outside.
My cousin and I climb plush stair,
past landings, arches, swirls, gold pillars.
Red velvet drapes open to a dark cavern.
The usher leads us away from single men
to a cubicle three rows from the top.

A mile down, Martin and Lewis posture,
toy with a roaring audience.
Ilona Massey graces the stage in a voluminous gown.
Across a panoramic screen, Danny Kaye cavorts.

I'm twelve.
My cousin had to get married at sixteen.
She named her baby "Sally."
I notice she's crying
and I'm sick, pop corn bitter in my mouth,
mohair scratching my bare legs.

-34-

Ceremonies

For ten years, my mother struggles,
losing ground every day, and after my father dies,
she never leaves her bed.
I take myself to the dentist, carry messages to the butcher,
cook the rich egg custard that sustains her.

Her lifeline is a radio on a night stand near the bed.
The voices from that ugly brown box offer wonders:
bloodthirsty ants ravage the countryside, devouring every living thing.
Joe Louis beats Conn in eight rounds.
Together we sob at Roosevelt's funeral,
listen spellbound to MacArthur speak.

When the Cubs make it to the Series,
we live for the nasal tones of Bert Wilson.
I pace the floor; my mother twists the covers
for seven incomparable afternoons.

She misses both my graduations and when I marry at twenty-one,
she has been gone three years.
Boxes that speak murmur her name.

Remnants

Relatives gather at our third-floor walk-up.
In her will mother left my aunt
a full-length coat of whisper-soft seal.
My cousins get fifteen Oz books from the Wizard on.
Father's gold cuff links leave in Uncle John's pocket.

In closets after mother's funeral,
I find father's silk umbrella, vicuna overcoat, worn slippers
lost since his death nine years before.
I throw them out, along with mother's bed jacket,
lingerie, junk jewelry, Oxfords.

Good Will carts off beds, tables, lamps,
a prickly mohair sofa, its matching chair.
I ask friends to hold the Sterling, settings of Limoges,
the chiming grandmother clock.

Their wedding rings, her antique locket,
rosary, necklace of "real pearls" go into a vault
along with his pocket watch, platinum tie pin
and the savings bonds, their death certificates.

-36-

Last to go is an Oriental carpet,
blue-gold diamonds across flaming scarlet.
I played for hours on it, raised towers of dreams,
childhood castles of multi-colored blocks.
On my eighteenth birthday, I sell the rug for fifty bucks
and tell Illinois Bell to disconnect the phone.

Roomers, 1940's

Iron twists three stories up to our five room apartment:
brown cement floors, naked light bulbs,
a kitchen table where I sit, listen to streetcar rumble,
laughter of men coming out of bars,
the click of the heavy Venetian blinds moved by hot wind,
my mother's weak voice on the telephone.

I sleep on a sofa in the living room where I can hear her call.
A flowered screen hides me from the strangers
renting our bedrooms by the week,
passing by me on their trips in and out.

Helen, braids tied in a bun, teaches me to inhale,
what drink to order on a date.
I eat lunch with Leonard, the accountant
whose fiancee visits his room Saturday afternoons.
When Nilo takes me on his lap, I am surprised by wet kisses.

Mother's dying cannot stop
my growing up on the other side of her door.

Part Three

Love, she thought, would bring her back.

Cleopatra Mathis

The Defiant Rose

for Anne Hutchinson

England, 1634

She abandons the graves of her daughters, lace curtains, bone china,
to follow God's wind across the Atlantic.
The ship rides low in the water, as many cattle as people.
When waves batter the decks and timbers splinter,
Anne leads the fearful in prayer.
William, husband and disciple, does not understand his wife
but senses the Lord addresses her.

-41-

Boston, 1636

The seven month child is breached hip-wise.
Mary Dyer howls like an animal.
Anne eases the dead fetus from her womb,
a mouth with bloody flesh protruding,
claw toes, horns instead of eyes.
Consoled by a gentle breeze,
she buries the creature, hastens back to Mary.

1638

Pregnant for the thirteenth time, age forty-six,
Anne stands before the court of scowling elders,
God's voice roars in her ears.
Hours later the verdict: "Leave Boston or hang as a witch!"
She clutches her stomach.

-42-

At dawn she moves into the garden,
ignoring sounds of hurried packing,
children crying like wounded sparrows.
She touches a favorite rose, its bare branches.
A thorn bloodies her thumb.
She will not see it flower again.
She wants it to flame, each blossom defiant.

A gale at their backs,
the family labors through snow-frozen drifts.
At night Anne rests her heavy body,
adds twigs to the fire,
prays that beasts will stay away,
natives not find them.
At the end of the journey, her dead baby is born.

Cumberland. June, 1642.

One day while Anne and William are kneeling together,
the boards of the cabin vibrate.
Sun fades to green light.
An ashen shaft divides the sky.
As the tornado takes the roof,
William reaches for his wife, falls,
his heart still.

-43-

August, 1642.

Two Mohawks startle Anne by the river
as she sings hymns, teaches Bible stories to the children.
She recognizes one man as a beggar she gave bread and milk.
Today his face is twisted like a gargoyle.
He bloodies two of the boys with a hatchet,
not seeing baby William crawl into the bushes,
William, who will one day father children,
a dynasty to last two hundred years.

The other Indian rushes toward her oldest daughter.
Anne hurls herself between them.
A powerful wind rises, tunnels through the clearing,
lifts her as easily as a stray petal
into heaven.

-44-

Ruins

Ellie, remember the jungle-edged ruins
we walked together, husbands ahead,
and the Mayapan sun that pressed us into
doorways, any slant of shadow.
Your Robert marched, collar ironed crisp;
back home he worked six days, puttered
with the cycle, raced the flats.

Uxmal,
we sat on crumbling altars,
eating oranges, giggling; it was
Christmas, hot. Who needed presents,
you said, money was just fine;
Robert, grinding his heel in a burial pit.

On Cozumel beach, windblown, biting nails,
you confessed: the island hadn't helped.
Robert was a stranger, and you were going
back to that little Kansas town, the only
redhead in ninety miles.

I chance on your address today and write.
Hoping you're not there.

-45-

South Portugal

For years I carried a snapshot
of you near an ancient crumbling wall
in south Portugal. The picture was all
I had. My need has creased the paper,
your face is cracked beyond hope of repair.

Today I learned of the death of another
man I loved. In time all memory grays,
but now I am numb like the night we kissed
goodbye in Lisbon. I drifted to the plane,
not swallowing, keeping your taste alive
until after take-off, the climb to clouds.

Surrounded by Water

Picture an airplane landing
on a runway just the length
of the land, wheels touching
near bloody fish hanging from hooks.
The terminal may be a grass shack
or a sock waving in the breeze.

The jungle comes right up to your room,
yellow hibiscus arranged on the pillow.
The hotel pool is a blue square in palms.
At night insects batter the screens.

Within a few days you will remember
an island is an isolated speck.
When you begin to yearn for traffic, T.V.,
and a week old newspaper,
you will remember the only way out
is by boat or plane
and understand why the islanders
are shy and hide in corners.

-47-

The Hotel Palmilla

Imagine a beautiful woman on the veranda
overhanging a cliff. Below waves foam on rocks.
It is August, 120 degrees.
The hot wind presses her gown into the hollows of her body.

She leans over a railing of white lace
to glimpse her lover's boat,
his catch glinting in the late sun.
She dreams he ascends the stairs
to lead her in a wild, Latin dance,
to press her back hard against
the glittering blue and white floor.

Instead the surf splinters
his boat upon a bed of rock.
She falls for the stranger
who appears at his funeral.

Look! She paces now on the veranda over the sea.

-48-

Legends

I wanted to stay in Oz forever,
but the Wizard sent me back to Kansas
where the wind never stopped.

I lived in dreams at Stella's,
begging cigarettes from strangers.
Now my world is feathers and whiskey. Smoke.

Hitler said "The greater the man
the more insignificant the woman."
I was called Mother of the Country,
but millions of my children died.

Rhett told me to go to Hell.
I laughed. He didn't understand.
I'd been there for years.

I did not have time to stop for death.
My garden changed from green to gold to white.
"Is there more than love and death?" And night?

My father traded me for power, then Arthur's
weight on me night after
night, and not one baby born.
"Legends get cold at night," said Lancelot.

-49-

Sequences

A smiling woman with marceled hair
holds a baby in her lap, flowered dress
blending with rose garden.

She poses again, laughing,
before a lagoon filled with small boats.
She wears a cloche, ankle-length skirt.
The child, older now, plays near the water.

Ten birthday candles frame shining faces:
mother, child, their cheeks touching.
The woman's hair brushes a lace collar
covering her shoulders.

Mother and daughter stand before a Christmas tree,
the girl with patent slippers, a bow.
Her mother's hair falls in a soft bob,
eyes closed against the flash.

How clearly I see yellow skin, tubes
while the summer woman in flowing silk
is a stranger in an album.

50

Blueprint for Emotion

Sentinels around an open grave, we stood in April
chill. 21 rifles fired. A young soldier
swept the flag into the arms of a weeping
mother. Two jets dipped in a leaden sky.

My uncle survived Bataan, returned home
to drink and double-deal for ten more
years. Yet that cold morning, I cried for him,
tears I hadn't found for my father.

How emotion tricks us after all.
With trumpets and uniforms, the pageant
manipulates, sucks us in.
Madame Butterfly sings, Cordelia suffers,
we cry,
yet dry-eyed endure the loss of hope,
an empty flat.

Butch Bond's Funeral

The whole county came but nobody cried.

Not Father Cogan whose sermon was short
because he'd never known Butch.

Not even Butch's mother, who had the energy
at ninety, to persuade Father that Butch had repented
in those last searing minutes.

Certainly not Butch's sworn enemies, smoking
outside the Church, muttering about the good men
Butch had outlived.

Lawyers hired to sue and subpoena,
the judges on the payroll and bartenders
and Butch's favorite whore sat dry eyed but admitted
they would miss the business.

-52-

Five Bond children did not cry
nor did other possible offspring
scattered around the Church.

His widow smug with survival and her secret
that Butch had not fathered their youngest
was deciding whether to keep the electric fence.
Before Butch, only small animals had been stunned.

Marriage in Three Acts

I

Bahama summers they swim through lazy days,
sip Margaritas at the pool. He licks salt from her lips.
Forgetting to eat, they collapse on pink sheets.
The day she hears a rumor at the Country Club,
she pitches her diamond at him. He flips it back.

II

She forgot his tux; they're late on New Year's.
He compensates with Absolut,
Cabernet Savignon at dinner, Chivas for dessert.
In feather-trimmed black chiffon, she whirls around the dance floor.
Midnight she looks for him, discovers he went home.

III

A Nile cruise marks their twenty-fifth.
When he snaps her, she offers a distracted smile.

Behind her, the Sphinx stares ahead,
nose crumbling, paws outstretched.

At the picture on their rec room wall,
he questions guests: "Was she ever that thin?"
"Which cat is oldest?"

54

Anonymous

He was bored by David, the Madonnas, The Annunciation.
Our guide asked him to accompany single ladies after dark,
but he appeared embarrassed,
sat in the lobby, watching
television in a language foreign to him.
Chain smoking, he clicked his lighter like a gun.

Elizabeth from Chicago pondered his soft, manicured hands,
his hearty "Good morning,"
but elusive small talk, the shabby black suitcase,
wallet without pictures.

One day the guide mentioned
a maid found him asleep, snoring
in the wrong room on a different floor.
His seat on the bus remained empty.

At first Elizabeth wondered where he was
but forgot by the time
the bus reached Sorrento.

-55-

Island Boy

He gets up late so he has to hurry,
dresses absently, his mind on the clouds,
the wind in the palms. She watches him
holding the baby, hardly recognizing her husband
with wild hair, frizzed at the ends.
He ties a sarong on one hip,
pedals into the mist.

All day he catches sharks for photographs,
helps women in and out of his boat.
Some nights he carries home a fish for dinner,
its scales reflecting late sun.

Most night he's at the bar.
Tipsy women manage to brush against his huge chest.
They buy him drinks. He smiles broken English,
ogles the heavy jewelry around their necks.
When he dreams, he dreams of gold.

56

Cairo, City of the Dead

At midnight we kissed under torches.
Now in a morning gray with mist,
I wave goodbye through dusty glass.
Tomorrow I will ache from edges.

The airport bus passes white buildings,
dead palaces crumbling into slum.
Centuries ago, priests anointed bodies here
when the Nile flooded the valley.

We cross bridges over a blue trickle,
desert yellow—sucking, winning.
Rain cannot save this narrow river.
I put out your eyes while their light is soft.

57

Definition

You ask about the shadowy man
who appears in Mayan temples,
wanders through Roman ruins,
skin dives off the beach in Tahiti,
buys me a beer in Madrid.
He darts out of dark alleys with knife drawn
or accuses from behind a screen.
No eyes under a wide-brimmed hat,
his calloused hands are gentle.

Enter the ghost I run from, the lover I desire,
the husband I compromise, the friend I betray,
the father I disappoint.
When I write him, he disappears.

58

Finalist

A certain compensation balances every gift and every defect.
Ralph Waldo Emerson

For years, I watched her dance,
head high, back straight.
Her mirror answered "fairest of them all,"
while I, shorter, plump,
seconded her slimness.
Sisters, rivals, she had grace
and I, mainly wit.

My body seemed to taut to sway:
I studied her instead, her graceful body turning,
full skirt swinging in, about long legs.
She whirled until her rhythms changed.
The drum beat on. Too proud to join the chorus,
she left the floor to me.

I eased her slippers on
without a fear of midnight.

0-595-21179-8